A
LETTER

TO THE

RIGHT HONOURABLE THE

LORD BROUGHAM AND VAUX,

CONTAINING

POPULAR REMARKS

ON

LAW REFORM.

By JOHN JENKINS, Solicitor.

Rem verò publicam nostri majores certè melioribus temperaverunt et institutis, et legibus.—
Cicero, Tuscul. Quæst.

LONDON:

S. SWEET, 1, CHANCERY LANE, FLEET STREET,

LAW BOOKSELLER AND PUBLISHER.

THE LORD BROUGHAM AND VAUX.

My Lord,

In looking out for an individual to whom to address the following remarks, on the *necessity* of a measure for a more prompt and economical administration of justice in this country, I found no difficulty in the selection. Your Lordship is pre-eminently entitled to be addressed on that subject. Your past services in the field of law reform merit it. In that field you have achieved much, and attempted more. The statute book of England yields honourable testimony to your services—its pages bear proudly the fruits of your labours. Whatever laurels you may have won in other spheres of enterprise, (and they, by universal confession, are many,) none sit more gracefully—none wave more gloriously, than those you have gained in the prosecution of law reform. The public rejoice to think that, though advanced in the vale of declining years, you have not sheathed your sword, but that you wield it now as mightily as in your days of pristine vigour. Yea, age appears only to heighten your zeal and strengthen your purposes. Go on in the career of law reform—more glorious conquests await you. No field more needs your cultivating hand—none is more suitable for you. The hopes of the public are in you—let them not be disappointed. You have lopped off many injurious branches : attack the trunk whence they sprang ; and substitute a tree, whose leaves shall be for the healing of the nation's wrongs.

Having premised thus much, I shall now enter upon my remarks. The delay and expensiveness of *law* are proverbial. Society in this country rings from centre to circumference with denunciation of its evils. In the minds of the laity law is associated with plunder, wretchedness, and destruction. Its practitioners are looked upon with greater suspicion and distrust, than those of any other legitimate profession or trade in the community. They are denied even the *ability* of acting justly, if they act *legally*. It is supposed that the successful practitioner has reached his hardly-earned position, by steps which are beside integrity—by means which social ethics, as well as christianity, condemn. Moreover, the proscription is universal—every member of the profession comes under the ban of condemnation. The lawyer is, in the public mind, indissolubly associated with unrighteous artifice, unholy purposes, and imposition. The character is wedded with insincerity. How comes the public mind to this conclusion? What are the steps by which it arrives at this goal? Can it be that the members of this profession are *naturally*, or even *actually*, less just or honest, and less under the influence of the great moral instincts of human nature, than other people? To suppose the first is absurd. The lawyer has not received from his Maker a heart more callous, or a mind more impure, than the rest of his fellow-men. He has the same human nature, and the same great principles influence his conduct. He is no anomaly in the great human race. The latter supposition is equally unsound and illogical. Can a profession change the nature, and reverse the principles of man? Is it capable of making the just, unjust?—the ingenuous, disingenuous? Could it make a William Penn unjust or an extortioner; or, a Howard the foe of his species? Evidently not. It follows then that the evil against which the public declaim is not in the individuals—the practitioners of the law. It resides elsewhere. Where can that be? Where is the fountain whence spring these deleterious waters? We are necessarily driven to the system—the machine, which the practitioners merely put into motion: we are forced upon the law itself. And here we are obliged to halt. We have absolved the lawyer from innate or actual corruption: we wish we could equally absolve his system. We confess we wish, and have strived to do so, but we also confess that after having fairly and maturely examined its claims, we are unable to pronounce it " not guilty." Its defects and evils are too palpable and grave to admit of justification, and the candid practitioner must admit the justice (to some extent) of the public's charge against his system—the law itself; although the same candour requires that he should firmly asseverate his individual innocence. Having then come to the conclusion that the law is defective and pernicious, we proceed to point out some of its principal evils, and will afterwards make suggestions whereby (in our opinion) they might be remedied partially, if not wholly. It is not our intention to discuss the general merits and demerits of the theory and practice of the law. Such an inquiry would embrace too large a compass for our limits. We leave unscathed the domain of conveyancing, and the law of real property. We will confine our remarks to what we consider the more glaring and tangible evils of legal procedure, and this principally as it affects the public in the recovery of comparatively small debts and rights. What we mean by small debts and rights are those, the amount or value of which does not exceed £50. And, afterwards, we shall throw out a few hints for the amendment of other branches of the law. The diseases which we shall expose are, we think, capable of an easy and safe remedy.

It is a truism that the present machinery for the recovery of debts and rights by legal procedure, is productive to the suitor of *excessive* expense and delay. To investigate the causes of this will be our present business. We apprehend that these evils may be traced to the following, as their principal causes; viz.—*First*. That the proceedings are mostly or partly conducted in London, or, in other words, that the principle of centralization is carried to excess. *Secondly*. That those proceedings are too numerous and complex; and, *Thirdly*. That the tribunal before which the case will ultimately be decided is too expensive, and sits at too long intervals, to which last may be added, that the place of trial is too far distant from the locality where the parties and their witnesses reside. We conceive that all the principal evils of the present system of legal procedure may be traced to one or more of these causes. We shall consider them in order.

First. That the proceedings are mostly or partly conducted in London, or that the principle of centralization is carried to excess.

Under the present system the greater part of the preparatory proceedings (as well as others) in an action are taken in London, at a distance, it may be, of two hundred miles, and upwards, from the residence of the parties and their attornies. There the greater part of the expense is incurred. The London agent's charges form, generally, the weightier portion of the client's bill of costs. The agent, the counsel, and the officers of the court abstract the bulk of the costs. Nor, in any case, are these very light or trivial; in many cases they are enormous. They are such as often necessitate the country attorney, even in successful cases, to charge the extra costs, or those costs in an action which cannot be recovered from the opposite party, against his own client; the effect of which often is, when the latter is the plaintiff, that the greater part, if not the whole, of the debt or damages recovered, is consumed, and the poor client is deprived of the fruits of his victory. The country attorney is frequently obliged to do this in justice to himself; if he should not do so, his labours might be unrequited, or at any rate be underpaid. If, on the contrary, the client be the defendant in the action, then he has the poor satisfaction of having to pay a considerable sum to vindicate his innocence, even where his opponent—the unjust claimant—is able to pay the whole. In this manner the successful party in an action runs a very great chance of being an actual loser by the result; while it is a matter of certainty that he will be deprived, to some extent, of the full fruits of his conquest.

The question then suggests itself, Is this system of centralization necessary, or, are its proved evils counterbalanced by advantages peculiar to itself? We think both members of this question may be safely answered in the negative. We think there is no greater necessity for having the various documents and proceedings (which are required in an action) prepared and taken in London, than there would be for the country grocer getting his pounds of sugar ready weighed and folded up, or for the country druggist having his doses prepared in the same great metropolis. The only possible advantage, in either case, would be that the article transmitted savoured of London. Essentially its superiority must reside only in name, in the bare advantage (if such it be) of having had a London birth. Absurd would be accounted the man who would undergo the trouble, delay, and expense of procuring an article from London, while he could have one equally good, and at less cost, in his own town. Equally absurd is that system which necessitates the suitor in a court of justice to undergo the expense and delay of having every document prepared, and every step taken in the same metropolis, while they could be done equally well, and at considerably less expense, in his own town or vicinity.

It is true there are local tribunals, called County Courts, throughout the kingdom, in which proceedings may be taken and documents prepared, without the necessity of their issuing from London. But the jurisdiction of these courts being limited to the trivial sum of 40s., joined to the fact of the great delay and irregularity which occur in their proceedings, renders them comparatively sterile as courts of justice. Probably the sum of 40s. was, in the reign of Edward the First, when the jurisdiction of these courts was limited and settled, equal in value to £25 at present. Still, though this kingdom has in wealth, population, and commercial greatness, outstripped even the wildest reveries of the founders of County Courts, no extension has been made in these tribunals to meet the advance. Surely the *boy's* suit cannot clothe the *man*. In many of these courts the long period of nearly three months must elapse from the commencement to the close of a lawsuit, even where it is undefended, before the creditor or claimant can have judgment for his demand. During this time the defendant (who is generally of the lower ranks of life) may get rid of his goods; yea, may sell them, and eat and drink the produce.

The constitution of these courts is also as objectionable as their proceedings are irregular. The undersheriff for the time being is the county clerk, or judge of the court. He, being invariably an attorney, is, in many cases, interested in the very cause, on the trial of which he has to preside as judge. His partialities and bias are still more extensive. We have also known instances (not few) in which the county clerk or judge of the court carried on more actions in his county court during his year of judgeship, than at any other time. But then, he loyally conforms to the law, and devoutly preserves his judicial independence and purity, by carrying on the proceedings in the *name* of a friend. Thus he gravely deals out the most Athenian justice with the one hand, while he scrapes the emoluments of a partisan attorney with the other. A parallel to this must be sought for, we think, among the darkness of the past, or the uncivilised of the present.

It is, moreover, true, there are in some places other local tribunals, such as Courts of requests, whose jurisdiction is much greater than that of County Courts, and where the suitors are free from the necessity of having their proceedings stamped with a metropolitan dye. But then, these courts are confined to comparatively few districts in the kingdom, and are mostly of recent creation. Their history, moreover, proves the utility, and entire subserviency to accomplish their ends, of local judicatures, whose proceedings are never touched by the magic wand of London.

Secondly, that the proceedings in an action are too numerous and complex.

Your Lordship is well aware that generally in a simple action for the recovery of a debt of three pounds, the entire round of special pleading may be gone through; including declaration, plea, replication, rejoinder, surrejoinder, rebutter, and surrebutter, with the attendant satellite, the demurrer. Several or all of these expensive processes may be used, and often *must* be used, in an action of the simple description mentioned, equally as in one where the subject matter involved is of the value of £10,000. Each one of these processes, with its attendant charges, often amounts to the best part of £3. What is the professed object of these expensive proceedings? It is to inform the parties—plaintiff and defendant—of the complaint on the one hand, and the intended defence on the other. Another object is to develope the points in dispute, to set forth the proposition or propositions affirmed by the one side, and denied by the other. Do they fulfil these objects?

It is well known to your Lordship, that the first mentioned object is frequently not at all, or very inadequately answered. The same words, with the exception of names, dates and figures, are used to represent cases that are as widely different in nature and substance, as the complication and diversity of human affairs can produce. The form of a declaration in trover is fresh in your Lordship's memory. So that if a person having lent or hired his horse to another, and the latter should take him away and sell him. If the owner should bring an action against the buyer, the law of England obliges him to state his complaint as follows; viz., that the owner casually lost the horse, that the buyer, by some chance, found him, and converted him to his own use. But I need not multiply instances. Your Lordship is well aware, that the cumbrous formulæ and the technical and mystic phraseology of special pleading, are ill calculated to inform the respective parties, of the several grounds of charge and defence.

It cannot be denied that the latter object, viz., the development of the real points in dispute, is, in many cases, partially attained by the present system of pleading, by reducing the number of witnesses, who would otherwise be brought forward to meet every imaginable turn of the case. But it is equally certain that this advantage is far more than counterbalanced by the attendant evils; viz., first, the great expense of the proceedings themselves; and, secondly, by the rules which confine the party—plaintiff, or defendant—strictly to the points made by him in his pleadings, and exclude other and more real grounds of complaint or defence. So that if a party's counsel or attorney should, in drawing the pleading, miss the proper point or ground, the client pays the penalty of learned error, by the loss of his case, and the disastrous expense which usually follows.

Moreover, the law of England itself *assumes* the uselessness of special pleading in cases that are of more importance than the recovery of a debt, or the acquisition of damages, viz., in the procedure of its criminal courts. There generally, yea almost universally, the only pleading consists of the indictment, which charges the prisoner with the offence, and the simple plea of "guilty," or "not guilty," uttered *ore tenus* by the accused. Seldom or never do the pleadings extend further. No voluminous and intricate pleadings are gone into, which oppress the memories of the judge, counsel, and attorneys, while they puzzle the unsophisticated minds of the jury. Surely if special pleading be necessary in a case where the simple question is, whether one party owes to another £5; it must *a fortiori* be necessary in a case where the question to be determined is, has a subject forfeited his life, by a breach of the penal laws of his country? If it be necessary in the lesser thing, it must be so in the greater. Its inutility in the latter shows conclusively that it is not necessary in the former. That the absence of special pleading from the general procedure of our criminal courts, lessens not its usefulness, no one better knows than your Lordship. Your great experience must have convinced you that the want of a long plea, replication, or rejoinder, on the trial of a prisoner, frustrates not the ends of justice. The same experience must also have convinced you that those ends are often defeated, by the application of the rules of special pleading to the solitary document, which is generally used on that occasion—the indictment. Often does special pleading unlock the door, whereby the thief or the man-slayer escapes to his former haunts of spoliation and crime—its absence never compromises the innocent accused.

Thirdly, and lastly, on this head;—that the tribunal before which the case is ultimately decided, is too expensive and sits at too long intervals; and, that the place of trial is too far distant from the locality, where the parties and their witnesses reside.

Your lordship knows that all actions of tort, and those arising from contract, where the claim is above £20, must be tried before the judge of a superior court, at the assizes. Those actions founded on contract, where the claim does not exceed £20, may, with few exceptions, be tried before the undersheriff, or other judge of an inferior court. So that an action, where the claim is £21, must be tried at the assizes. The counsels' and court fees, on the trial of such an action, generally amount, on each side, to about £20. This is exclusive of the witnesses' expenses. The latter being added, generally make the *costs of the day* of each party, on the trial of an action for the recovery of £30, or under, much exceed the amount sought to be recovered. The effect of this upon the litigant parties generally, is, that the action is settled or compromised before trial, in order to avoid such enormous expense and risk. Yea, it often necessitates a party to take the half, and even less, of his just demand, to escape such heavy responsibility. Such is generally the case, when his opponent has not sufficient worldly goods to answer the sum to be recovered, and the costs; or, it is apprehended, that in case of ill success the losing party will dispose of his effects before execution can issue. Yea, not unfrequently a party discontinues his suit altogether, and consents even to pay his own and his opponent's costs, rather than face a trial at the assizes, with its ponderous charges, while he would unhesitatingly have tried it before a less expensive tribunal. The effect of this system, as regards poor clients, is frequently an absolute denial of justice. In such cases, the attorney often prudently declines carrying the case to trial, unless a sum sufficient to answer the day's outlay, is placed in his hands. This sum is generally £20. If the client cannot find it, his case is untried, and he has the melancholy satisfaction of losing his debt or demand, and of being liable to the payment of the costs on both sides.

With regard to the next branch of my proposition, viz., that the court sits at too long intervals; it is well known that the assizes for the trial of civil causes, are held only twice a year. Then, only, has the class of actions which we have been discussing, a chance of being tried. The interval between the spring and summer assizes, is generally about five months, and between the latter and the former, about seven months. So that generally three or four months must elapse from the commencement of an action, before it can be tried; and, in other cases, seven or eight months. During this time the hands of justice are tied up, the litigant parties are in a state of corroding anxiety and excitement, while the suit drags its slow length along, acquiring, daily, an aspect more serious, and a bulk more ponderous, from the additional charges which adhere to it by the way.

The last part of my proposition is, that the place of trial is too far distant from the residence of the parties and their witnesses.

The assizes, it is well known, are held in one town for the disposal of the business of the county. *There*, the parties and their witnesses must attend, and, when they chance to reside in a remote part of the county, the distance is often great. By this means the expenses of conveying the witnesses, and of their maintenance, are often very great, forming a very imposing item in the bill of costs. The distance of the witnesses' residence from the assize town is frequently forty miles. The expense of their conveyance and maintenance would be about £5 per head. So that should there be only four witnesses on either side, their expenses would amount to about £20. Where the distance is greater, or the witnesses are more numerous, the expense is, of course, proportionally increased. Hence, it is evident that the witnesses' expenses on the trial of an action at the assizes, are frequently so great, as to call for very strong reasons to justify so enormous an outlay. In fact, it shows the extreme desirableness of having justice administered nearer to the doors of the litigating parties, if such a course be practicable.

It is true, as we have before stated, that most actions arising from contract, wherein the claim does not exceed £20, may be tried before the undersheriff, or other judge of an inferior court, but generally before the former. This was, doubtless, a boon (such as it was) to the public. But though, in those cases, it cheapened justice, it did not, by any means, improve its quality. Most of the objections which we have before urged against the judicature of county courts, apply equally to the sheriff's courts. The undersheriff is the judge, and he invariably is a practising attorney. He carries into the judgment seat the bias and prejudices necessarily arising from his situation. It would be expecting too much of human nature to think otherwise; to suppose that the moment he enters the judicial chair he leaves his frailties behind. Unfortunately these charitable suppositions are too seldom verified in practice. We ourselves have been the painful ear-witnesses of an undersheriff's charge to the jury, which (as was evident to all by-standers) was deeply tinctured with party-bias and predilection. The mere power to perpetrate, and inducement to pursue such conduct, should not be allowed, by the enlightened legislature of a free country, to desecrate the venerable precincts of a court of justice.

The cardinal evils produced by the system which we have been discussing, are *excessive* delay and expense. The consequence as regards the public, is for the most part an invincible dread of the law. Few comparatively have the courage to commence an action at law; fewer still have the fortitude to carry it to trial, if resisted. Many would sooner forego their rights, be they ever so certain and clear, than embark in a lawsuit, whose consequences are frequently so disastrous. Perhaps, generally, it is only the irresponsible and the reckless who are anxious to plunge into litigation. The timid, the prudent, and the man of substance, are generally deterred from even touching " the hem of its garment." By this means, frequently does the dishonest debtor treasure up the wealth of another, and the trespasser and libeller feel secure from the rod of retributive justice. The injured party mourns over the wrong which he has received, but looks with dismay at that law which offers to him its help; while the wrong-doer enjoys the fruits of his misconduct, and rejoices at the thought of the impunity which that law secures to him. The poor man regards the law as an article which it is beyond his power to command; and sorrowful is his heart, when he thinks that his enjoyments are at the mercy of his rich neighbour. The latter tramples with indifference on the rights of the former, knowing that he has a longer sword on the battle-field of *law*. The philanthropist observes these things with bleeding heart, and sighs to see such injustice and inequality in the world; while the speculatist despairs to trace their existence to any other source than the selfishness and perversity of man.

The evils then of the present system being certain, the question presents itself, can they be removed? Can a better one be substituted? We conceive that these questions may safely be answered in the affirmative. We pretend to no new discovery, we profess to offer no fresh nostrum. We shall but advance old truths—but promulgate old plans. These may appear in a fresh garb, or may receive some slight additions from our pen, but their identity will remain.

We confess, my Lord, that the remedy we propose for these evils is a Local Courts' Bill—such a bill as, with some modification, has often heretofore been presented by your Lordship, and others of your noble and learned compeers, to the notice of Parliament. The leading features of those measures are well known to your Lordship. They provide for a division of England and Wales into districts, to be presided over by judges of fitness and respectability. That these districts should be divided according to the number of the inhabitants they contain. That there should be one or more judges to preside in each of the large towns of England, while one judge would suffice for several counties of small population. That the station and salaries of the judges should be such as to insure their respectability and fitness. That they should hold their courts (of course public) according to the wants, and to suit the convenience, of the population of their districts; those whose districts comprise only one large town, to sit daily (with, of course, all reasonable exceptions), while those appointed for country districts should make periodical circuits, and hold their courts once a month, or otherwise, in each important town and place in the district. That these courts should have all the necessary subordinate officers to carry on the proceedings with efficiency and promptness. We would propose that their jurisdiction should extend to all debts and demands not exceeding £50. Moreover, that they should have jurisdiction over all actions sounding in damages; such as trespass, trover, case, and detinue, where the damages claimed by the particulars of demand, or the value of the article sought to be recovered in *specie*, does not exceed £50, as well as to actions for the recovery of sums certain. Their jurisdiction might also be usefully extended to certain descriptions of ejectment; ex. gr. to cases between landlord and tenant. We presume that the court, which is competent to decide an intricate case of assumpsit, would be also competent to try an action of trespass or trover, or even a simple case of ejectment. That the judicial tribunal at these courts should consist of the district judge and a jury of six or more individuals, as at present in trials before the sheriff. That these courts should decide according to the common and statute law of England, and not according to *equity and good conscience.* That there should be a Court of Appeal from the decisions of the District Courts, on matters of law, in order to secure uniformity of decision. That the scale of fees for transacting business in these courts should be sufficiently liberal to induce professional men of respectability to practice in them. *Lastly.* That they should be invested with all the requisite powers for regulating their proceedings and enforcing their decisions.

The proceedings in an action in these courts we propose should be simply as follows. That the plaintiff, or his attorney, should make out a plain business-like statement, in writing, of his demand or claim against the defendant, with a notice at the bottom, informing him, that unless he will comply therewith by payment of the sum (if money), or restitution of the article (if goods), with payment of the costs, he is required to appear at the next or other practicable sitting of the District Court to be held at a certain time and place (specifying them), to answer the complaint. Let this statement of claim and notice be served on the defendant, in due time before the sitting of the court at which he is summoned to appear. Should the defendant intend to resist the action on any special ground of defence, such, for example, as a bar by the statute of frauds, of limitation, gaming, usury, &c., let him be required to deliver to the plaintiff, or file at the court, a week or so before the sitting at which the cause is to be tried, a statement in writing of such intended ground of defence. If the case be not settled in the mean time, let the parties—plaintiff and defendant—attend at the time and place mentioned, with their counsel, advocates, and witnesses (if any), and the trial commence and be conducted in the same manner as a trial at the assizes, or as near as circumstances will admit. Should either party be dissatisfied with the decision for error in *law,* let him have a right to go to the Court of Appeal to be heard thereon.

Your Lordship will have observed that the foregoing outline differs in two important particulars from most other plans which have been hitherto proposed. These are, first, in subjecting these courts to an observance of the *law* of England, in the same manner as the superior courts now are; and, secondly, in establishing a Court of Appeal from the decisions of the local tribunals. We think these two additions would be most important amendments.

First. As to obliging the local tribunals to decide according to *law.*

The public have a great prejudice against that law, which is made by the magistrate or judge, at the time he pronounces a decision founded upon it—they have an invincible dread of that functionary, who unites the characters of legislator and expounder of the law. They do not like to subject their lives, liberty, or property, to the will, caprice, or even good conscience of any *one* man. They like to know the law by which they will be tried, the rule by which they will be judged. They think there is greater security for the enactment of *good* laws in a hall of senators, than in the judgment seat. They have a deep reverence for *the law of the land*. They think that its mantle waved over their birth, and that under its shade they have hitherto walked—under its tutelage, therefore, they wish to journey through life.

Secondly. As to establishing a Court of Appeal from the decisions of the local tribunals.

The object of this would be to secure uniformity of decision and procedure among the various local courts. This is of the greatest importance in the judicial administration of an enlightened and highly civilized country. It would be anomalous and highly objectionable, that one description of law should be administered in county A., and another in county B. In such case the law would vary according to territorial limits. The subjects would then consider that the guilt or innocence of their conduct depended much on the locality where they abode, or the court which took cognizance of their acts. They would think that the conduct which received condemnation from Judge C., might be exculpated by Judge D. Hence the necessity of a Court of Appeal from the decisions of the local tribunals, to secure uniformity of law in their adjudications. Moreover, by this means, one of the strongest objections on the part of the opponents of local courts, viz. the probable want of uniformity in their decisions, would be removed. The right of appeal would, of course, be confined to alleged errors *in law.* The present practice of our courts, confining the dissatisfied party to a decision to appeal on *matters of law,* is founded on the wisest experience, viz., that the court which hears the evidence from the lips of the witnesses, is the most competent to decide on the *facts* of each individual case.

Furthermore, we think that if our suggestion as to allowing a scale of fees sufficiently liberal to induce professional men of respectability and competency to practice in the local courts, were adopted, another most potent objection on the part of the opponents of such tribunals would be removed. The objection we refer to is, that in such courts, where the scale of professional remuneration was low, respectable practitioners would be alienated from them, and the practice would be engrossed by the irresponsible and the mean; or the proceedings might be conducted by the parties themselves; in which case, they say, the scenes of irregularity and confusion observable in our police courts, would be witnessed. A liberal allowance to professional men, for proceedings conducted in the local courts, would effectually remove these objections.

The observations which have been made, respecting the present evils of legal procedure, are, of course, confined to *an action at law*. They are with fourfold force applicable to a suit in Chancery. An action at law represents but in miniature the expense and delay, which occur in a Chancery suit. According to the petition of the solicitors of the court presented in 1841 by Mr. Pemberton Leigh, (then Mr. Pemberton,) £1,000 is the smallest sum which justifies the institution and prosecution of a suit. In all cases where the sum, or the value of the subject-matter involved, is less than that amount, (and are they not many, yea, the most?) a suit is not warranted; and there is consequently, in an immensity of cases, a denial of justice. The doors of the court of Chancery are closed against the poor man's suit; yea, the substantial and honest yeoman often finds it difficult to make his prayer heard; and then, the higher walks of life are frequently desolated by the disastrous effects of Chancery litigation. How often is a Chancery suit in a family seen to strip the ancestral mansion of its magnificence, the walks and avenues of their beauty, the garden of its luxuriance, the servants of their livery, the carriage of its splendour, the farm-stead and cottage of their wonted trimness; and how frequently the scene closes with insolvency and the auctioneer's hammer! Aptly did your Lordship quote Dean Swift (in your memorable speech on the amendment of the law), who represents Gulliver's father "as ruined, by gaining a Chancery suit with costs."

The delay occurring in Chancery proceedings is also enormous. An action at law may generally be terminated in four or six months, while a defended Chancery suit trails through an existence of so many years. The suitor in Chancery has frequently to look through a long vista of anxious years, before he shall enjoy the fruits of his victorious suit; yea, it may have been commenced in youth, while, before its final termination, his head may be streaked with the gray of age. Many a care-worn suitor, unable to bear the ponderous load so long, sinks prematurely into the sepulchre of his fathers.

Surely a remedy is wanted for this state of things. These courts should be more in reality what they are in name, viz., courts of equity. Then may we expect the public to be more reconciled to the law, and have better faith in its practitioners. But whatever may be thought of a radical change in the constitution and procedure of Chancery, with respect to claims of considerable amount, or value, it is certain there is a crying necessity for a prompt and economical administration in equity cases, where the amount of the claim, or the value of the subject matter in dispute, is less than the sum named, £1,000. The fact that at present there is no *beneficial* remedy for such cases establishes this *necessity*. No one is better able than your Lordship to devise a plan to meet the wants of this case; and may we be permitted to hope, that such a measure will not be tardy in following the introduction into Parliament of a Local Courts' Bill, to meet the defects of the present procedure in courts of law? Perhaps the jurisdiction of the proposed Local Courts for the determination of *legal* cases might be usefully extended to such equity cases as we have last described. Apart from the consideration, that *abstractedly* there is no difference between a so-called legal claim and an equitable one, and assuming the present division by our legal code to be well-founded, there appears to be nothing incompatible in the junction of the two jurisdictions. We cannot see that any "war of elements," much less any "crush of worlds," would follow such a union.

The next subject to which I beg to draw your Lordship's attention, is that of Bankruptcy and Insolvency. Your Lordship is aware, that under the late acts legislating on these subjects, England and Wales are divided into districts, which are presided over by commissioners. When the measure was originally announced, the disinterested portion of the profession looked to it as a boon, and the new courts were regarded as decided amendments on the old system. It cannot be denied, that these anticipations have been, to a great degree, realized, so far as concerns the *quality* of the administration dispensed. The courts are more public, the commissioners more competent, the officers more independent and less liable to sinister influence, and the proceedings altogether are conducted with greater efficiency and promptness. But it must be confessed, the expense of working a fiat in bankruptcy has not been diminished: on the contrary, it has in most cases been increased. The reason of the greater expensiveness of bankruptcy proceedings at present we conceive to be, that the courts are stationary—being held in only *one* town in the district; where all parties, whose attendance is necessary, must go. In many districts, to our knowledge, the parties to a bankruptcy or insolvency are obliged to travel above a hundred miles to attend each meeting. The expense consequent upon this in a bankruptcy, must be considerable. Generally speaking, small estates are entirely consumed, by the joint grasp of the landlord's rent and the bankruptcy expenses. Unless the estate produce more than

£200, the creditors might as well look for "grapes off thorns, or figs off thistles," as for a dividend on their debts. This expense is confessedly excessive, and operates most injuriously on the interests of the commercial world. Then, what is the remedy? We conceive, that to make the courts ambulatory would be effectual. We would propose, that the commissioners and the subordinate officers should make periodical circuits, (once a month or otherwise,) through their districts, and hold courts at some central town in each county. By this means, the travelling expenses of the parties to a bankruptcy or insolvency would be generally much lessened, which, under the present system, is the canker that devours small estates.

I would next call your Lordship's notice to the law of Evidence, which appears to have already received your Lordship's attention, from a bill which last session you introduced into Parliament, entitled, " An act to enable parties to be examined on the trial of Civil Actions;" and the speech by which it was accompanied. Your Lordship is reported to have said, " No interest, however great, in the event of a suit, was sufficient to exclude a man's relations. Why not examine the parties themselves? This was done in the Court of Chancery; why not in the courts of common law, under due restrictions?" This, my Lord, was a bold statement of an important truth—a truth that has been often iterated by some of the greatest of modern jurists. The gratitude of the public is due to Lord Denman, who, by the Act, 6 and 7 Vict. cap. 85, removed the brand of incompetency from interested parties (other than those to the suit nominal or actual); and from individuals who may have been convicted of crime. This act wisely provides, that any objection to a witness, on the ground of interest or crime, should be directed to his credibility, and not to his competency. This measure was a great advance in modern legislation, and was dictated by a spirit not less noble than enlightened. It is one of those acts which serve to brighten the otherwise dull pages of our statute-book. This distinguished fellow-labourer of yours, and companion in the walk to greatness, has, by an effort worthy of himself, removed a portion of the rock which obstructed the free current of truth in the channel of evidence; it is for you, by an effort equally worthy, to demolish the splinters that remain.

We shall now proceed briefly to examine the objection urged to the admission of the evidence of the parties themselves on the trial of an action. Probably the following would be a fair statement of the objector's argument;—that the object of legal investigation is to arrive at the facts of a case,—that the interest of the parties to the action is such as in all probability to so far influence their testimony in favour of themselves, as to lead them to perjury,—therefore their testimony had better altogether be excluded. We fully admit the premises, but dissent from the conclusion. It is undeniable, that the object of legal investigation is to arrive at the facts of the case; it is also undeniable, that the interest of a party to the suit is such, as *generally* to influence his testimony in his own favour—*frequently* to the extent of perjury; but we think there is an intermediate question to be solved, before the conclusion stated follows. That question is, Is it not better to present before the judge and jury the testimony of *all* witnesses to the facts of the case, interested and disinterested, that they may compare, analyse, and weigh the evidence on both sides, and give credence to that which preponderates; than to exclude the testimony of the parties themselves, who are in *most* cases the *best* witnesses, and in *many* cases the *only* witnesses, of those facts. By admitting the testimony of the parties themselves, no other description of testimony is excluded. All other sources of evidence are as accessible and available as before; you only let more in, possibly dangerous testimony, but one which would in all cases be regarded with suspicion, and, when conflicting, would only be credited so far as it received corroboration from internal or external facts. Where one party would affirm, and the other deny that affirmation, the judge and jury would primarily consider the matter as if there were no evidence to the point on either side; but then, they would inquire further whether there were any other evidence, internal or external, which showed the greater veracity of the one testimony than the other. Should such be found, it would, of course, sway their decision. We will illustrate our meaning by an example. We will suppose that A, a watchmaker, sold B, a merchant, a gold watch, and having sued the latter for the price, he should plead the statute of limitation—that the debt was contracted more than six years before the commencement of the action. A would first be examined, who would swear that the watch was sold five years and a half before the commencement of the action; B, on the other hand, would swear that the sale took place *six* years and a half before that time. If it should further be proved that B was publicly proclaimed a bankrupt a little more than six years before the commencement of the action, the probability would be, that A would not have trusted B for the price of a gold watch so soon after his embarrassments; consequently, that the watch was sold before that event, and therefore more than six years before the commencement of the suit. In a similar case the corroboration might be in favour of A's testimony, by his showing an authentic ledger, in which was entered at the time the sale of the watch, on a day within six years; while B could produce no written entry in confirmation of *his* version of the case.

But this is reasoning on a supposition the most favourable to the objector, and the least favourable to ourselves, *i. e.*, on the assumption that the parties themselves would go into court determined to swear anything, or everything, to gain their own ends. We hope as strongly as we believe, that, notwithstanding all its weaknesses, human nature is not so sunken, as this supposition pourtrays it. We believe that, generally speaking, man is not so lost, nor so dead to the moral sentiments of his nature, as to be able, in the presence of his Maker and his fellow-man, deliberately to asseverate falsehood, because it might happen for the time to answer some sinister end. No, we think, there is

"Some remnant of the Angel still,
In that poor *Being's* nature;"

at least, enough to preserve him from a state so hopeless and depraved as that supposed. Yea, we think, that be their interest on the score of *money* ever so strong, (as in the instance of the parties to actions being witnesses,) men, by force of the dictates of their inner nature, combined with the sanctions of law and public opinion, would frequently, nay generally, in such situations, speak the truth. Exceptions, no doubt, there would be, and those numerous and potent, but the *rule*, we believe, would wave on the banners of truth.

Again, the difficulty of the generality of witnesses stating and *supporting* a falsehood in a court of justice, under the searching cross-examination of the adverse advocate, and in the presence of a public assembly, is confessedly great. It has been well said, that one falsehood requires a file of others to support it. More particularly is this the case in a court of justice, where the inventive faculties of the witness would be taxed to the uttermost—(to perhaps an extent that would generally end in an explosion of the fabricated story)—in coining fresh falsehoods to give strength and coherence to his first aberration from truth. One discrepancy in the tale would be likely to expose the nudity of the whole—one breach in the rank of *alleged* facts, to throw the mass into inextricable confusion and rout. Add to this the motives to veracity created by the law of the land. Few men are found so obdurate or callous as to mount the perjurer's box, in the face of transportation beyond the seas, or incarceration within a prison's walls. But it may be answered, many have done so, and many are continually doing so. Yes, but charity would lead us to hope, as experience would induce us to believe, that these are the excrescences of the moral world.

Upon the whole, we think, that notwithstanding the great danger of admitting the evidence of the parties themselves on the trial of actions; still, it would be accompanied by so many countervailing advantages, that to legalise such testimony would in the end be conducive to the interests of justice and truth; and that *he* will be a benefactor to his kind, who will bring this consummation to pass.

I would, lastly, call your Lordship's attention to the state of the law as regards the landlord's rights, and his remedy for the recovery of rent.

The landlord's rights in regard to rent are an anomaly in our law—his remedy for its recovery stands isolated in our system of jurisprudence. They are both encroachments on the policy of the rest of our laws. Should a tenant become bankrupt, insolvent, or be subjected to an execution, the law carefully provides for the payment of a year's rent to the landlord. *He* must have the choicest part of the pie, though his knife was latest in it. He may have slept in serene and pampered security, while some poor tradesman, (whose *all* was in the tenant's hands,) has passed wakeful nights, until the law, (after tardy and expensive progress,) has given him a right to seize the tenant's goods, towards the satisfaction of his debt. He no sooner makes the seizure, than lo, an awful discovery is made—a year's rent is due to the landlord; and he, with lordly gait, at the twelfth hour, steps in and demands his rent. There is no escape—his title is wrought by Act of Parliament, and a denial would be visited with "pains and penalties" of law. One of two things must be done—either payment of the year's rent, or abandonment of the levy. The former is of course done, where there is an adequate surplus after payment of the rent; but the latter alternative is painfully submitted to in those cases (not few) where the rent fully or nearly equals the value of the goods. The poor tradesman then mournfully turns away from the scene of his disappointment and loss, and often is he heard to denounce that law, which makes such distinctions where none should exist, and which pampers one class of the community, while it depresses and cripples the energies of the rest.

If in these cases an arrear of years should be owing to the landlord, and if before the sheriff's officer enters and seizes the goods, the landlord, his agent, or bailiff, has the forehand of him, and merely says, "I distrain these goods for the rent," the lien, as by electric power, is unalterably fixed; and the favoured son of the law rejoices in the thought that his entire rent shall be paid, even before the poor execution creditor realizes a farthing to pay his costs.

Moreover, the landlord's remedy for his rent is an exception to the policy of the rest of our law. Everywhere else it loudly proclaims, that every man should have an opportunity to vindicate his innocence or honour, before the claim is enforced—that no one should take the law into his own hands—that no lynch law shall be tolerated on the green sods of the British isles. All these maxims, which are but different expressions of the same great principle, are wantonly violated by the landlord's distress for rent. How often the power is used as an engine of injustice and oppression, I need not say; suffice it, that the right is as unfounded in principle, as its exercise is often replete with tyranny and wrong.

The public have a right to ask, Is that debt which is due to a person on a contract for the use and occupation of a house, or a field, higher in nature, and entitled to precedence, over a debt due to another person, for a supply of the necessaries of life? Is the one debt sacred, and the other profane? Does the one contain ingredients of a more elevated character, as to deserve priority in rank and station? Is it a more heinous offence to withhold payment of the one than the other? These are legitimate questions, and until they are fairly answered, and the landlord's prerogative is shown to be founded in reason, the public will continue to regard it as a usurpation, and its exercise as an invasion of their plainest rights.

I need not inform your Lordship that the law we have been last discussing is a relict of the feudal system, and stands prominently forward among its modern remains, to dishonour the jurisprudence of our land. The more hideous parts of that system have long ago been consigned by the legislation of St. Stephen's, or the advancing surge of the national mind, to the grave they deserved; and it is high time that this lingering remnant of mediæval barbarism should follow the fate of its kin.

I have now done, my Lord, and I feel that an apology is due, for the length to which my observations have run. Perhaps, also, my reasons for coming out and assailing some of the venerated institutions of our father-land will, in some quarters, be exacted. The moving cause was neither avarice nor ambition, neither the desire of fortune or fame. I have written because, I have *felt*—I have felt because I have *seen* in the walks of actual life the evils, which in the foregoing pages I have attempted feebly to delineate. I think I may venture to assert, that the preceding remarks are the offspring of experience and well-considered facts. And here, permit me to say, my Lord, that I think the practising solicitor or attorney has better opportunities of testing the merits and demerits of the practical part of the law, than the barrister, or even (with deference do I speak) the Judge. The latter, generally, only see in perspective the results of litigation on the homes and the happiness of the parties themselves—they have but *a priori* glances of the scenes which follow the termination of a suit; it is *he* that is the road-side companion of the parties from the beginning to the end of the march; and it is *he* who is the eye and ear-witness of the joy or the sorrow—the gladness or the grief—which is the sequel to the conflict's close. *They* conclude that the loss of an assize trial by a weak tradesman, or of a Chancery suit by a not opulent yeoman, must be followed by disaster and woe; but it is *he* who is called in by the hapless suitor, and his circle of family or friends, for advice and assistance to avert the impending blow, and to find for the disconsolate man, and, possibly, some helpless objects of his affection and care, the best refuge from distraction and want, until the storm shall have sped and past.

Respectfully craving your Lordship's attention to the foregoing remarks, and hoping that, should they contain any new or undiscovered suggestion which may meet your Lordship's approval, fitting use may be made of it, either by incorporation into some measure which your Lordship may present to the notice of Parliament, or for aid in debate, or otherwise, as your Lordship shall think proper.

I have the honour to remain,

My Lord,

Your Lordship's most obedient, humble servant,

JOHN JENKINS.

August 20th, 1845.

P.S. Since the greater part of the foregoing remarks were written, my Lord, an Act has passed "for the better securing the payment of small debts." The original bill—of which the provisions for extending the jurisdictions of existing courts formed no part—was a good measure, laudable in design, and perfect in execution. We are sorry we cannot award the same praise to the provisions which were subsequently annexed. If this portion of the Act was intended for "a local courts' bill," it must be admitted it is a most imperfect one. Its object appears to be, to remedy the evils of the present law for the recovery of small debts and rights, by enabling Her Majesty, with the advice of her Privy Council, to extend the jurisdiction of existing local courts "to all debts and demands, whether on balance of account or otherwise, or damage arising out of any express or implied agreement, not exceeding £20." It is very doubtful whether county courts, hundred courts, and baron courts, are extendible under this Act. The court which appears to be capable of enlargement, is one, having an " Act constituting any such court ;" while, it is well known, the courts we have named were not constituted by statute, but exist by the common law. If this be the true construction (and the whole wording of the Act seems to favour it), this measure furnishes but a very scanty and partial provision for the wants of the community, as the courts we have named, are to be found in every part of the kingdom; while those created by statute, such as courts of requests, are confined principally to its large towns and populous districts.

Moreover, the provisions of this Act are very inadequate as regards the courts, whatever they may be, which come within its purview. Provision is made for the appointment of a judge where there is already no qualified one, but not a *word* prohibiting him from practising at the same time, either as counsel or attorney ; not a *word* prescribing the mode of proceeding in these courts ; and not a *word* on many necessary subjects besides. In short, the whole business of providing for the establishment of Local Courts is disposed of in about a dozen short and badly-worded sections—a less number than is generally devoted to the unimportant details of a Dock or Railway Act; and the little that is being encrusted, like an oyster, by the shell of an Insolvency Bill. Surely the legislature having by this measure admitted the existence of the evil, but having provided a palpably inadequate remedy, has now no escape from passing a " Local Courts' Bill," that will, we hope, be as comprehensive in design, as full in detail, and otherwise complete in execution.

J. J.

G. H. WARD and Co., Printers, 16, Bear Alley, Farringdon Street, London.